Oh Baby!

The A to Z

Kane Miller
A DIVISION OF EDC PUBLISHING

Aa
adventurous
anteaters

are always

looking for

ants.

Bb
bear

Cc
chicken

is curious about flying.

Dd
donkey

Ee

elephant

is running
to swim with his friends.

Ff

fox sees something up high.

Gg

goat is tired from a busy day.

Hh

hedgehog

has a very spiky hairstyle!

Ii
impala

Jj

jaguar

can't wait to
be one of the
big cats.

Kk
kangaroo

L l

leopard

Mm
marmoset
worries about tripping
over his tail.

Nn

newt

love to swing!

P p

pig

Qq

quail

Rr

racoon is clever with his claws.

Ss
sea lion

want to dance all day.

Uu
upland geese

V v

vulture

shouldn't be sad.
Mom will be back soon.

Ww

wild boar

is waiting for her dinner.

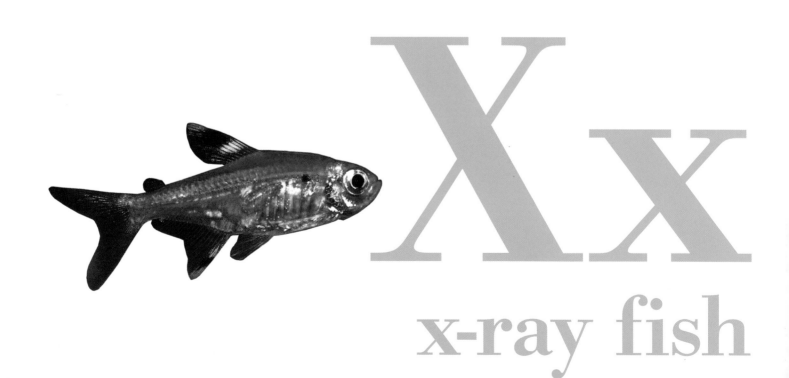

Xx

x-ray fish

Yy

yak

Zz
zebras

can't stop zipping around.